Hinkemann. A Tragedy
Ernst Toller

HINKEMANN
A TRAGEDY

By Ernst Toller

Translated from the German
by Peter Wortsman

New York and Berlin, 2019

Hinkemann. A Tragedy
By Ernst Toller

Translated from the German by Peter Wortsman
Translation Copyright © 2017 Peter Wortsman
This printed edition Copyright © 2019

Berlinica Publishing LLC
255 West 43rd St., Suite 1012
New York, NY, 10036, USA

ISBN USA: 978-1-935902-52-2
ISBN ebook: 978-1-935902-98-0
ISBN Germany: 978-3-96026-035-6
LCCN: 2018956678

Cover: Eva C. Schweitzer

www.berlinica.com
blog.berlinica.com

He who has no strength to dream,
Has no strength to live.

Hinkemann, A Tragedy is the first book of a new series of German and Austrian plays in translation presented by Berlinica Publishing. The series will present authors such as Bert Brecht, Kurt Tucholsky, Karl Kraus, and Walter Hasenclever, but also post-war authors such as Rolf Hochhuth. Ernst Toller's *Hinkemann* is the first volume to appear.

Characters

Hinkemann
Grete Hinkemann, his wife
Hinkemann's mother
Paul Grosshahn
Max Knatsch
Peter Immergleich
Sebaldus Singegott
Michael Unbeschwert
Fränze, Grete's friend
Stall holder
Various male and female workers
All kinds of people off the German street

Time and Place: Circa 1921, Germany

Translator's Note

This translation previously appeared on the website The Mercurian, *in Fall 2017.*

I have chosen to keep the character names in the original German, though each name has an ironic allegorical significance, as in a kind of Everyman *play.*

Hinkemann might be translated as Lame Man. Grosshahn as Big Mouth or King Cock. Knatsch is German slang for trouble or quarrel, thus his name might be translated as Max Quarrel. Michael Unbeschwert might be translated as Michael Easygoing, Immergleich as All the Same, and Singegott as Sing God's Praises, or Mr. Amen.

ACT ONE

Scene One

Implied setting: The kitchen of a working class apartment that also serves as a living room. Grete Hinkemann putters about at the stove. Hinkemann enters. Sits down at the table. His right hand rests on the table clutching a small object. He stares steadfastly at the hand.

(Hinkemann speaks neither with ease nor with pathos. His manner of speech retains the awkwardness, the heavy muffled tone of the elemental soul.)

GRETE: Did mother give you the coal?

HINKEMANN: (*Doesn't answer.*)

GRETE: Eugene!... all I asked was if mother gave you the coal... Answer me, for god's sake... As if he weren't even here!... Eugene, say something!... I can't stand it! Not a single piece of wood! No coal! Eugene, should I light the oven with our bed?

HINKEMANN: A tiny little creature... a pretty colored little thing... its heart beating like wild... I can feel it. Trembling in the night. In the endless night.

GRETE: What've you got in your hand, Eugene?

HINKEMANN: How can you stand there so cool and collected? Don't the pots fall out of your hands? Don't you feel a giant darkness closing in on you? A little creature of the earth, like you, like me… still so glad to be alive… tweet-tweet-tweet… And now! Now! I got there just as she was poking its little eyes out with a red hot knitting needle… (*Groaning*) Oh! Oh!

GRETE: Who? Eugene, who?

HINKEMANN: Your mother. Your flesh and blood mother. A mother! A mother blinding her pet canary with a red-hot knitting needle, because she read in some rag that blind birds sing more sweetly. I threw the coal down at her feet, and the ten Marks she gave me, Grete… I… I beat your mother the way you beat a child that tortures animals… But then I let go… I couldn't help thinking… it was a terrible thought, Grete, terrible! Wouldn't I have done the same in the old days? Without batting a lash? What did the pain of an animal matter to me then? An animal, so what! Twist off its neck, poke it full of holes, shoot it dead. Who cares? I was healthy then, and this all just seemed the way things had to be. Now I'm a cripple and I know: It's awful! It's killing your own kind. Worse than killing! To be tortured alive!… But before!… The healthy man's blind to it all!

GRETE: What have you done?… It's hopeless.

HINKEMANN: Can you imagine: for a mother to blind a living thing! I can't believe it! It's awful! I just can't believe it!

GRETE: (*Leaves the room.*)

HINKEMANN: My poor little bird… my little pal… what have

they done to us, you 'n me? People did it. People. If you could speak, you'd call devil what we call people! Grete!... Grete!... Gone, huh? Bored of our company, I guess. (*Searching around the room for something.*) Breadcrumbs... a cage... a cage? So that one of us can show off his pain to the other?... No way! I can't be cruel. I'll play the hand of fate. A fate kinder than my own. You see, I... I love you... my little friend...
(*Hinkemann runs out. Comes back again after a few seconds.*) Blam! A red spot on the stone wall... A few feathers flying... finished!... A thought—and the whole world totters! If they'd've shown me somebody like me before, I'd've... I don't know. There are times when you just don't know what you'd do, that's how little you know yourself... Maybe I'd've laughed... yeah, I might've... laughed! And she... Her mother poked a canary's eyes out... Ya know what she's gonna do?
(*Laughs hysterically. Sings out in a shriek:*) Ah... ah...

(*While Hinkemann sings, Grete enters the room, stares at him, afraid. As though with a shudder of disgust, she presses her hands over her ears. Suddenly she lets out a piercing sob.*)

GRETE: Oh, my God!... Oh, my God!

HINKEMANN: (*Notices Grete, turns to her in a fit of rage.*) What's the matter, woman... what the hell are you crying about!... Answer me!... What are you whining for, huh!... Huh!... Crying 'cause I can't... 'cause people'd point at me like a clown, if they knew? 'Cause some goddamn sonofabitch took a pot shot and turned me into a pathetic cripple... a laughing stock? Because you're ashamed of me?... Tell me the truth... the truth... I'm dizzy... I'm so dizzy... I've got to know the truth. (*Pleading desperately.*) Why are you crying?

GRETE: I... I love you...

HINKEMANN: Do you love me... or is it pity makes you tremble when you hold my hand?

GRETE: I love you...

HINKEMANN: There was an old dog on his last legs... we used to play with him when we were kids... he was a good creature, such a fine, faithful friend... a dog that couldn't stand to see anyone lay a hand on us... and then one day he got the mange. His fur got all scruffy, his eyes ran... you couldn't touch him anymore without feeling sick... except, you see, except that you remembered the way he used to be, the way he'd look at you with those human-looking eyes of his, and the memory, even then, when all the joy was gone... the memory... you just couldn't let them take him to the pound... and so you tolerated him in your room... and you even let him crawl into your own bed... (*With a shriek*) Grete! Is that what I am?... a mangy old dog?

GRETE: (*Holds her ears shut in despair*) I can't stand it anymore! I'll find a rope!... and I'll turn on the gas!... I can't stand it anymore!

HINKEMANN: (*Helplessly*) Gretchen, what's the matter? I'm not doing anything to you. I'm a lost man. I'm a hidden disease. I'm a rag doll they tugged at so long till I came apart... This pension's not enough to live on and just too much to die... Gretchen, I'd betray my own pals, I bet I would... I'd go and be a scab, if... if only... if only it didn't choke me and choke me... you see, here, it sits in me like a pin cushion, jabbing and jabbing: you're nothing but a mangy dog to your wife...

(*Quietly, secretively*) And Grete, since today, since I saw that at your mother's, since I had that thought, that terrible thought… it's been hounding me, hounding me… I hear voices… faces glare at me… a gramophone sits in my throat, like some ghastly animal growling its song in my ears: Eugene's a joke! Eugene's a joke!… And then all of a sudden I see you… you're standing in a room all alone, you're standing at the window, I'm walking down below… you're hiding behind the gardenias… and your lungs… your belly's bursting with laughter…
(*After a while, simply*) Gretchen, it isn't true, tell me, you couldn't laugh at me, you couldn't do that to me, could you?

GRETE: What do you want me to say, Eugene? You don't believe me anyway.

HINKEMANN: Yes, I do! I do believe you, Grete! Ah, Grete, I'm in heaven! I believe you!… I'll find a job… even if I have to grovel like an animal!…

(Paul Grosshahn enters.)

GROSSHAHN: Evening, everybody.

HINKEMANN And GRETE: Evening.

GROSSHAHN: What's all the fun about? Tell me, I could use a good laugh.

HINKEMANN: You, Paul? Haven't you got plenty to laugh about? You've got a good job. Why you'll probably make foreman pretty soon.

GROSSHAHN: Foreman, my ass! It's pull in your belt for the bosses and layoffs for us. Poor people're worse off than animals. Least they get fattened up and sent out to pasture till they're round enough for the butcher's knife.

GRETE: It's a sin to talk like that.

GROSSHAHN: How can a poor man sin? If there were a hereafter, we'd've earned our seat in heaven—first, because we were so busy hustling to survive we had no time to sin, and second, it's only fair payment, seeing as we built them their heaven on earth... Besides, I'm an atheist. I don't believe in God. Which one should I believe in? In the Jewish God? In the pagan God? In the Christian God? In the French God? In the German God?

HINKEMANN: I bet they all got tangled up in barbed wire... the holy tacticians.

GRETE: My whole life long I've kept my faith in God's justice and nobody can take that away from me.

GROSSHAHN: If God was just, Mrs. Hinkemann, his actions'd have to be just too. And how does he act, this kind, just, loving God of yours? Huh? Do I need to tell you? With God for king and country, with God for mass murder, with God for money and power. All of it's God's will... almost seems sometimes like when the bosses'd rather not, when they're ashamed to say "I," then they say God instead. It sounds better ... and the people are more likely to fall for it... I leave faith to those who profit from it. We're not fighting for some heaven above, we're fighting for the earth, we're fighting for mankind.

HINKEMANN: Fighting for mankind, that's alright with me... but for the machine... it breaks your bones before you even get up out of bed. I dread every working day, and when I start work in the morning I can hardly imagine keeping it up all day. Then evening comes, and I hear the bell and storm out the gate like a lunatic released from the asylum.

GROSSHAHN: Machines don't bother me. Me, I'm the master, not the machine. When I stand at the throttle, I'm rarin' to go. You've got to let that sucker feel you're the boss! And then I drive that howling, humming, moaning gizmo till it won't give no more, till it sweats blood... in a manner of speaking... and I laugh because I love the way it whines and buckles under. So, my little pet, I cry, yours to obey, do or die! And I feed it the wildest hunk of wood, and make it carve according to my command! My command! If you're man enough, Eugene, then you're the boss!

HINKEMANN: (*Quietly*) There are times when it's easier to act the God than to be a man.

GRETE: (*Stares fixedly at Grosshahn*) What a wild look in your eyes, Mr. Grosshahn.

GROSSHAHN: Och...

HINKEMANN: I'll tell you one thing, he didn't learn that look from no machine.

GRETE: Where?

HINKEMANN: Where? Gallivanting with the ladies, that's where.

GROSSHAHN: What's life to us poor folks? The moment you land in this life the old man starts cussing that there's another mouth to feed. You go off hungry to school in the morning, and when you get to bed at night the hunger's still gnawing at your gut. And then you join the work force. Sell your strength like you'd sell a gallon o' gas. And you belong to the boss, the man with the money. And you become... in a manner of speaking... a hammer or a chair or a steam shovel or a fountain pen, or else you turn into a laundry iron. That's the way it is. What's the one joy you have left? Love! Where nobody can tell you what to do? Love! Where you're free on home ground and you can tell the boss and his flunkies: Private Property! No trespassing! Love! The rich, see, they've got so many things to amuse themselves with... seaside vacations and music and books... but us? Yeah, sure we pick up a book once in a while, but not every day. Who's got the know-how? Who's got the time? And music? Well, opera's alright, but gimme a good variety show or an operetta... "Marquis of Luxembourg"... or "Waltzing Dream" or "The Merry Widow,"... you know the... (*Singing*) Vilja, o Vilja, sweet maid o' the woods"... or lemme drop a dime in the juke box, play a waltz and grab my girl... that's my idea of fun... To us, love ain't what it is to the rich. It's our... in a manner of speaking... it's our reason for living. If that goes, you can just as well can it all. Ain't it the truth, Eugene?

HINKEMANN: Maybe so.

GROSSHAHN: You're a married woman, Mrs. Hinkemann, I don't have to beat around the bush with you. What's life if a guy can't be with his girl at least once a day?

HINKEMANN: (*Watches Grete intently*)

GROSSHAHN: What do you say, Mrs. Hinkemann?

GRETE: I'd say... (*Timidly*) ... not all women are alike.

HINKEMANN: (*Jumps up*) I'll find work, Grete, you can bet on it... gotta get you a little something for Christmas, now don't I...

GROSSHAHN: Don't waste your time.

HINKEMANN: We'll see, Paul, old buddy, we'll see! Bye bye, sweetheart!

(Hinkemann leaves the room. A few seconds of silence.)

GROSSHAHN: What a man!—All muscle and bone! Damn shame he's got to lie around doing nothing. And always laughing. You must be very happy, Mrs. Hinkemann?

GRETE: (*Stares with a blank expression*) Uh-huh.

GROSSHAHN: You know, I'm always jealous of Eugene when I see the two of you together.

GRETE: (*Bursts into tears, drops her head into her hands.*)

GROSSHAHN: What is it, Mrs. Hinkemann?... Did I say anything wrong? You're crying... what is it? Shall I run after Eugene? I still might be able to catch up with him...

GRETE: (*Weeping uncontrollably*) My head is cracking open! They can cart me off to the mad house! I can't stand it!... I can't stand it!

GROSSHAHN: (*Concerned*) Are you ill, Mrs. Hinkemann? Can I help? Or are you expecting? Is that it? Some women get dizzy, you know.

GRETE: Oh my god, oh my god… if only. (*A burst of hysterical laughter*) …if only they'd come and bury me today…

GROSSHAHN: Is Eugene mistreating you? Does he beat you?

GRETE: I have to… I have to… I have to tell… what a miserable creature I am… my Eugene… my Eugene… my Eugene's not… he's not a man at all…

GROSSHAHN: You sure you're not ill, Mrs. Hinkemann? Maybe you got a fever?

GRETE: Nah… my Eugene… my Eugene, they did it to him in the war… and now he's a cripple… I'm so ashamed, I… I can't explain it… oh please understand, Mr. Grosshahn, he's not a man anymore… (*Shocked at herself, she holds her hands over her mouth.*)

GROSSHAHN: (*Gives off a short raw burst of laughter.*)

GRETE: Oh my God… what have I done? You're laughing at me like… ughh!… ughh! I never thought you'd… I never thought you could be like that.

GROSSHAHN: I'm sorry, Mrs. Hinkemann, it's just that… it just came rolling right out. A man hears that sort of thing, he's gotta laugh. (*Aghast*) But that Eugene, what an egotist! What's he holding onto you for? He doesn't love you, if he did, why, he'd let you go…

(*Grosshahn caresses Grete. Grete leans against him.*)

GRETE: It's so much harder than you think, Mr. Grosshahn. There's no telling what will happen from one moment to the next. First it's light and then all of a sudden it's blackest night again... I feel so sorry for that man... what a man he was before the War! A man in the bloom of life! But now... all he can do is brood. He quarrels with God and quarrels with people... and when he looks at me, it feels like he'd like to see right through me, like I was a thing, not a human being. And sometimes, I'm afraid of him... and I can't stand him being near me... he makes me sick!.. (*Shivering*)... he makes me sick! Oh Lord Jesus Christ, how will it all end?...

GROSSHAHN: (*Ever more tender*) You just cry, Ms. Grete, you just cry. Tears held back are like stones on the heart. My mother, god rest her soul, always used to say that.

GRETE: You won't tell him, will you, Mr. Grosshahn? I'd drown myself!

GROSSHAHN: I won't say a thing, Grete. Mum's the word. You can count on me. I did a month in the clinker once just 'cause I swore to keep my mouth shut... you can rest easy on that account. You know, you're still a young woman... look at me, will ya! Christ you won't last another year if you go on like this... Greteken... Greteken... (*He kisses her.*)

GRETE: So I'm a bad apple now...

GROSSHAHN: Bad? Nothing natural is bad, nothing... in a manner of speaking... of the blood. Bad, that's a word the preachers and money-bags like to bandy about. You'd be bad to yourself if you stayed faithful to a man who's not a man. What's faithfulness anyway? A silly old wives' tale to the rich. A friend o' mine, he had a thing going on with... the wife of a minister of state...

GRETE: I hear somebody on the stairs... what if it's Eugene...

GROSSHAHN: Then I'd better be going... Greteken... maybe you'd like to come and see me some time? You know where I live, don't you... don't have to worry, nobody's ever around... you can pour your little heart out to me... in a manner of speaking... you can have yourself a good long cry... will you come then?

GRETE: I don't know yet...

GROSSHAHN: Greteken, you still remember how we used to build sandcastles together in the big sand box in the park? I had my eye on you back then when you still ran around in pigtails... Greteken... will you come and see me?

GRETE: (*Shakes her head reluctantly.*)

GROSSHAHN: (*Suddenly brutal*) Don't you get coy with me now! You're coming!

GRETE: I...

GROSSHAHN: You're coming!

GRETE: Yes...

GROSSHAHN: Goodbye then, Greteken... see ya soon... (*Grosshahn leaves.*)

GRETE: (*Alone*) I'm just a poor woman. My life is so mixed up.

Curtain

ACT TWO

Scene One

Implied setting: The façade of a green carnival wagon. The impresario sits on a tree stump amidst carnival equipment. Hinkemann stands in front of him.

HINKEMANN: (*Points to a newspaper ad.*) Here!

IMPRESARIO: What... here!--?

HINKEMANN: It says here: (*Reads slowly emphasizing each word*) "Strong man wanted for sensational act. High pay. Only the best need apply."

IMPRESARIO: So that's what you're here for. Let's have a look, my friend. (*Inspects Hinkemann*) Biceps... spongy... chest... thighs... calves... spongy. Just what I've been looking for. Big soft muscles like a bear. Prima! Primissima! Hired! It's a deal!

HINKEMANN: And what do I have to do?

IMPRESARIO: Ah yes. Child's play. Pay attention! The people, my friend, are a flock of sheep. Pacifist nonsense. No business sense. The people want blood!!! Blood!!! Two thousand years of Christian morality be damned! I give them what they want. So you see, the public good and private enterprise work hand in hand. Capisce? No childish illusions, of course. (*Reaches for a flute.*)

What's this?
(*Plays a few notes on the flute.*)
Old hat! Syrupy sweet! Sentimental schmaltz! Ughh!...
What's this?
(*Grabs two drumsticks. Starts beating a big drum.*)
What is it?
(*Drumroll*)
Folk music!
(*Drumroll*)
Delirium!
(*Drumroll*)
Ecstasy!
(*Drumroll*)
Life!

HINKEMANN: You were saying?

IMPRESARIO: Patience, my boy, patience! Here a cage of rats! Here a cage of mice! Small fortune to be made. All you do at each performance, bite off the head of one rat and one mouse. Lick a few drops of blood. Wave good-bye! Basta! Finished! And the crowd howls with delight!

HINKEMANN: Living animals?!... No, Sir, I can't do it.

IMPRESARIO: Nonsense! Eighty marks a day. Free food. Fifty minutes work all in all... sensitivity aside, my boy! Nothing but a matter of habit. And think of the fringe benefits! The women, Sir, hot on you tail. Scruples aside. Surgical magic can repair a woman's lost virtue nowadays. There are medical specialists for that.

HINKEMANN: (*Greedily*) Eighty marks...

IMPRESARIO: Change of heart? Ha... ha... ha...

HINKEMANN: It's awful... lit..tle... li... ving creatures!...

IMPRESARIO: Go find another job then, Sir. Good luck! Ha... ha... ha! It's either-or!

HINKEMANN: (*Gulping*) It's... just... that... my... wife... (*Coughing it up*) If somebody loves you! And you're scared you could lose that little bit of love! Love's so hard to come by!... Couldn't you use my service in some other way, Sir?

IMPRESARIO: Either-or!

HINKEMANN: (*Stammering, almost whimpering*) Eh... eh... eh... eh... eighty marks. Nowadays... nowadays... gotta turn like a carousel to survive. Gotta keep turning! Gotta keep turning!... I'll do it, Sir.

IMPRESARIO: Now you're talking! Kings, generals, pastors and impresarios, we are the real politicians: We grab the people by their balls!

(*Stage goes dark.*)

ACT TWO

Scene Two

Faint candlelight. The silhouettes of Grosshahn and Grete flash on the rear wall.

GROSSHAHN: Love me?

GRETE: You, only you.

GROSSHAHN: And Eugene thinks...

GRETE: Stop! Forget about Eugene! I hate him, hate him!

GROSSHAHN: Strange, you womenfolk... why didn't you leave right when he got home... soon as you found out?

GRETE: Oh, I don't know. I don't know anything anymore... I think I was ashamed in front of the others.

GROSSHAHN: Poor guy, really, when you think about it.

GRETE: Don't think about it. I don't want you to.

GROSSHAHN: But Eugene's my friend, after all.

GRETE: Stop it! Stop it!

GROSSHAHN: Say, what was it like the first night? Did he try to?

GRETE: Oh Paul... shut up!

GROSSHAHN: And what if he was healthy, would you still come to me?...
(*Pause*) ... Why'd you get up? What're you doing?

GRETE: God strike you dumb! And me. And him! And everyone! In the beginning was the word... and the word was hell!

ACT TWO

Scene Three

Implied setting: An Amusement Park.
The façade of a booth with garishly painted walls that drown out the roar of the crowd.
Organ grinder's music. Trombones. On the stage in front of the booth stand a tattooed woman and... Hinkemann, who wears a flesh-colored body suit.

IMPRESARIO: (*In a snarling staccato*)) Ladies and gentle-men! Step right up... step right up! Listen! Look! At the amazing! Monacchia, the tattooed lady, with master-pieces from Rembrandt to Rubens... on the front... and the latest Expressionist, Futurist, Dadaist creations gracing her naked posterior! The lady will not only bare her legs, the lady will not only bare her back. She'll show you every square inch of skin permitted by the laws of church and state. Unnn-der eighteen not admit-ted. And as an extra special added attraction, you will witness the decapitation of an honest-to-goodness liv-ing child! You've never seen this before! You won't see it in Africa, you won't see it in Asia, you won't see it in Australia, only in America and Europe will you witness such wonders! And last but not least...
(*Pointing to Hinkemann*) ... Homunculus, the German Bearman! Devours living rats and mice before your very eyes! The German hero! The pinnacle of German cul-ture! The peak of German manhood! German strength! The darling of fashionable ladies the world over! Grinds

stones to powder! And with his bare fists alone pounds nails through the thickest skulls! With two fingers alone, ladies and gentlemen, he can strangle two hundred and thirty men! He who sees Homunculus must flee! And he who flees must die! You can't say you've seen Europe, if you haven't seen Homunculus! And you'll see more, much much more! You'll be thrilled by surprises—but let me not strip off the diaphanous veil of mystery. Therr-rre... forrrrre, without further ado, step right up! You won't pay a mark. You won't pay fifty pfennig. Today and today only, because of the enthusiastic turnout, you'll pay just thirty pfennig a head! Step rrrrright upp, ladies and gentlemen! Best seats are going fast! The band is about to begin! The artists are striding to center stage!

(A bell rings) Tickets! Tickets!

GIRL: (*Pointing to Hinkemann*) Hey, Teresa, get a load o' that hunk!

OTHER GIRL: Hubba-hubba-hubba!

IMPRESARIO: (*Who has overheard their remarks*) Give a touch, ladies! He ain't cardboard! He ain't paper maché! That's Homunculus, the incarnation of German strength!

(Enter Paul Grosshahn and Grete Hinkemann, arm in arm, in tender embrace. At first they don't look toward the booth. While they speak, the noise and the to-do in front of the booth is not audible. But the agitated gestures and movements of the crowd are clearly visible.)

GROSSHAHN: Isn't life beautiful, Grete? I'd like to whoop for joy! You wanna ride the merry-go-round, Grete? You can do anything your little heart desires.

GRETE: It must be a dream... just like a fairy tale... six years of heartache, trouble and misery. I sat shivering like a mouse in its hole, afraid to crawl out into the light. Not that I asked so much of life, Paul... don't think I'm like that... any poor girl knows from knee-high on what to expect. If things work out okay, it's a life of toil till you get old and you've got to lean on your kids. If things go bad, it's arguments, fights and beatings. But I never imagined things could turn out like this!...

GROSSHAHN: You're starting a new life now.

GRETE: (*Tenderly*) Oh, Paul!

GROSSHAHN: What, Grete?

GRETE: Paul.

(*Grete kisses Grosshahn long and tenderly.*)

GROSSHAHN: (*Smugly*) So much for modesty... in front of everyone... I told you so, didn't I... modesty... nothing but a word... in a manner of speaking.

(*The impresario's voice is heard.*)

IMPRESARIO: Homunculus, the German Bearman!

(*The voice fades.*)

GRETE: Paul! Paul!

GROSSHAHN: What are you yelling about, Grete?

GRETE: Look over there, Paul!... You know who that is?

GROSSHAHN: Who?

GRETE: The acrobat over there in the tights.

GROSSHAHN: How should I know him? Probably some traveling actor. Here today gone tomorrow.

GRETE: It's him.

GROSSHAHN: Who?

GRETE: Eugene!

(The impresario's voice is heard.)

IMPRESARIO: Devours living rats and mice before your very eyes. The German hero! German muscle! Homunculus, the man of thunder! Achtung, ladies and gentlemen!

(Hinkemann stands in a wrestler's pose and rolls his muscles.)
(The impresario's voice fades.)

GROSSHAHN: What a miserable swindle! That's the German hero! A guy with no… a eunuch… hahahaha! Maybe the German reservists looked like that! The stay-at-homes, the fat cats from Brussels, the newspaper simps, the war profiteers, the yes-men, the Herr von So-and-so's!… Hey, that impresario's turning cardboard into money!

GRETE: Shush up… be quiet… how can you be so heartless! And me, what kind of woman am I! I'm worse than a common whore… she sells her body, and I sell my husband…

GROSSHAHN: (*Clasps Grete tightly*) Cut it out! I'm sick of your sentimental crap!

GRETE: Didn't you hear it? He eats living rats and mice! That man wouldn't hurt a fly! That man once beat my mother for blinding her pet canary. He wouldn't let me set up a mousetrap in the kitchen... said it would be a sin to torture mice like that... and now he's eating them alive...

GROSSHAHN: So from now on you don't have to kiss him anymore!

GRETE: I'll kiss him... here... right here on this stage... in front of everyone I'll kiss him! What have I done to that man! The injury wasn't his fault! It was my fault because I let him go to war! It was his mother's fault! It was the fault of our time, that lets such things happen!

GROSSHAHN: Shut your mouth! People are already looking at us. Let's go! He might see you.

GRETE: Let him see me, in all my shame! I'll get down on my knees: God has forsaken me. I'm an insect in his eyes. Let go, let me run to him!

GROSSHAHN: (*Pressing Grete to him*) And if he makes you sick again?

GRETE: Then I'll love him all the more.

GROSSHAHN: (*Drags Grete along after him*) You're not in your right mind, woman! Let's go!

(*The voice of the impresario is heard.*)

IMPRESARIO: Right this way, ladies and gentlemen! See great wonders and surprises!

(The impresario enters the booth.)

WORKING CLASS WOMAN: *(To another)* So what if I happen to be taking these blouses to the pawnshop, that don't mean I haven't got any left... why I even own a fine silk mantilla that my grandmother left me... but there's nothing else left that's worth pawning... so these blouses'll just have to go...

(They walk by.)

(Grosshahn and Grete on the opposite side of the stage.)

GRETE: *(Still being dragged along by Grosshahn, but resisting)* N... no!

GROSSHAHN: You're not coming with me?

GRETE: No!

GROSSHAHN: And what if he notices that you're pregnant?

GRETE: He'll forgive me... he's good...

GROSSHAHN: He'll beat the hell out of you is what he'll do!

GRETE: So be it then... Now I see what God meant me for. God hasn't completely cast me off. God gave me a penance. I humbly accept it. I'll serve Eugene like he was my Savior.

GROSSHAHN: I'll go tell him... right now...

GRETE: Let's both of us go…

GROSSHAHN: And I'll tell him that you cheated on him…

GRETE: Why are you threatening me, Paul! I'm not coming with you. My life never belonged to me. When I was young I waited for life. Later I saw it from afar. But when I reached out to grab it, all of a sudden I thought to myself that I had such rough filthy hands, and life looked like it always went around decked out in silks and finery… and so I kept my hands buried in my apron pockets. How could I let them see my hands! Today I see that life is filthy too, and there's no use grabbing for it.

GROSSHAHN: (*His vanity injured, and therefore, extremely hostile*) Then you can go to hell, you simpering cow! There are plenty others where you came from… all I gotta do is lift my little finger… and they'll come flying like bees to a honey blossom…

(*They are shoved onwards by the crowd.*)

(*The impresario steps out of his booth. Hinkeman is with him.*)

IMPRESARIO: Ladies and gentlemen! Step right up! Step right up! Listen! Look! Be amazed!

(*The stage grows dark.*)

ACT TWO
Scene Four

Implied setting: Interior of a small working-class tavern. Behind the bar a lively proprietress serves with animated gestures. The customers sit at bare wooden tables. Max Knatsch, Peter Immergleich, Sebaldus Singegott and two anonymous workers, a roofer and a bricklayer stand at the bar. Angry voices are heard even before the curtain goes up.

ROOFER: And if there was a hundred revolutions! No revolution's gonna change a damn thing! Housepainter's better than a whitewasher, book printer's better than a wallpaper printer, typesetter's better than a boilermaker, high class chauffeur's better than a plain old cabbie. Roofers will always be roofers, and bricklayers will always be bricklayers.

BRICKLAYER: Get off it with your high and mighty horseshit! We sit at the same table with you! Even if we are mere bricklayers and no highborn roofers. We're bricklayers! And proud of it! Yessir! Bricklayers!

ROOFER: To work with slate, now that's an art. Anybody can lay a brick!

BRICKLAYER: We bust our asses same as you. There's no difference between us.

ROOFER: It's all a matter of skill, my friend. What was it like before the War? Wasn't our wage five cents more than yours? Isn't that proof enough? I'm a roofer, Mister, and I'll stick to my craft! If somebody even suggested today that I start laying bricks, why my youngest'd crack up laughing! My honor's unassailable, and no revolution's gonna change that!

(Both pay and leave. They continue arguing while leaving.)

BRICKLAYER: You overblown roofer!

ROOFER: Low-down bricklayer!

BRICKLAYER: Herr von Roofer!

ROOFER: Jealousy! Jealousy! You bricklaying blockhead!

KNATSCH: Solidarity of the proletariat! The enlightened proletariat. No difference among the proletariat—my ass!

(He notices Hinkemann, who has just entered and sat down at an empty table.) Eugene Hinkemann? What brings you here?

HINKEMANN: (*Short of breath, gruffly*) My throat was dry. I had a taste, it was like animal blood... an awful, bitter taste, parched my throat... had to have a drink... for God's sake, I'm not one of those teetotalers, that you need to be surprised to see me here!

KNATSCH: Surprised? Not at all! Why should I be surprised? Me, I don't need a bitter taste to get me to the tavern. All I gotta do is take a look at our kitchen at home, our salon-livingroom-laundry-storeroom all in one... take a look at our miserable kids... or even just think of my wife, that nagging old... and then I do a fast about-face on the stairs and run for my life... straight to the tavern...

We men aren't exactly innocent, I know. We're tongue-tied at home. Tongue-tied. At every political rally we shoot off our mouths to total strangers... and with our own wives at home we can't squeeze out a single word.

(While Max Knatsch speaks, Michael Unbeschwert enters.)

UNBESCHWERT: *(Has overheard the last few words, and starts in right at the door.)* Yes, indeed, happiness inhabits the palaces and villas nowadays. Where they've got twenty rooms and it's still too small for their liking. But I tell you, this War shattered the whole structure. It's already cracking, and you can see the chinks forming in the walls, you can see their knees shaking, the ones with a guilty conscience, the ones that can't fall asleep at night, you can hear their teeth clattering away in their pale faces. Comrades, I see the light of a new day!

(Sebaldus Singegott speaks up.)

SINGEGOTT: Your light's not the true light. Your light is nothing but a flicker before the gates of the heavenly kingdom. You seem to think that every worker's a soldier for your cause. There are many workers who seek their salvation elsewhere. That's what you people always overlook.

HINKEMANN: You speak of happiness, Comrade Unbeschwert. I've been thinking a lot about what happiness really is. And... you know... I came to the conclusion... that it's just not there for everyone... true happiness, I mean... that kind of happiness is something—*(Takes a deep breath)*—you've either got or haven't got it.

UNBESCHWERT: Bourgeois ideologies, Comrade Hinkemann. Your words really do sound a little ridiculous to me. (*With the pathos of a public speaker at a rally.*) The new society will be born in the wake of inevitable historical developments. Just as the Baltic and the North Sea quietly eat away at the shoreline—of which process we inlanders are simply unaware—so will our society grow into a socialist state, without us even noticing it. That's no phantasmagoria! There's scientific proof for it! And everything will work according to the party program. It's really very simple. Why should there be a lack of happiness? To begin with, we'll stop producing silk blouses, for the sake of a few lazy socialites, and we'll start producing cheap woolen blouses, so that those who have no blouses at all can be dressed and stay warm. Reason dictates its own conditions. In three words, comrades: A sensible humanity... and a sensible humanity leads to a happy life. In one fell swoop society will leap from a state of want to a state of freedom. It's really so simple.
(*Addressing Knatsch*) But those who think they can skip over historical stages—those radical fanatics and hotheads from the East, who would put belief in the place of science...

KNATSCH: The likes of us be damned, I know, I know. Since you people found the one and only formula. All you lack to be a preacher, comrade, is the cowl. Go ask the will of the People! If the People don't want revolution, then all your "historical conditions" won't mean a thing. And if the will to revolution is there, then any conditions are ripe seeds of the new beginning. Right now. This very minute. We don't need to wait for any special "conditions." But for you people! Obedience: Yes. Responsibility: No. And by the way, you always failed us when the time was right and called for action.

SINGEGOTT: Yours isn't the true light either, Max Knatsch. I saw the light, comrades. I saw the light and I rose up to meet it, the heavenly light.

IMMERGLEICH: It's all the same to me, just leave me my peace and quiet... don't take that away from me... or else!

UNBESCHWERT: You don't belong to any party, Knatsch. You're an anarchist... If you don't belong, then you have no sense of responsibility. There's no point arguing with you. Go join a party first! And you, Singegott, you're simply not enlightened, you're not class-conscious. I'll say it again: It's a matter of the right historical conditions! The rest is easy.

HINKEMANN: (*Answers Unbeschwert*) Maybe it is easy. A lot of what you say makes sense... about the woolen blouses and the silks... my sentiments exactly... man can't be noble if he's hungry... you've got to give him food and shelter first and a little bit of beauty before you can ask him to be virtuous... Maybe I'm too simple-minded to understand it all, to see it clearly, to grasp it all as you do... You're a party leader, you come to quick conclusions...
(*Since Unbeschwert feels himself under attack and evinces anger.*)
Not that I have anything against The Party. The bourgeois can never know what The Party means to the Working Man. For the bourgeois it's just The Party, nothing more. But for the worker... despite any blemishes... despite its imperfections... it means so much more. To The Party he brings his faith in mankind, it's his religion... but tell me... what if a man happens to be sick... sick in his makeup, sick inside, incurably sick... or externally sick, incurably... can any conditions make such a man happy?

UNBESCHWERT: I don't quite get what you mean.

HINKEMANN: I know, ever since my injury in the war, I admit that my thinking's a little off… Every day when I wake up it's so hard to make sense, to arrange my thoughts, to put it all into words, everything I've got whirling around in me, colliding, exploding, knocking against me and fumbling with my mind… Life is so strange… so much of what we go through we just don't understand, can't fathom, scares the hell out of us… you can't see rhyme or reason in it… you ask yourself, is it even possible to understand life… or is it like trying to empty out the ocean with a bucket… or like wanting to understand yourself? You just can't… all you can do is live through it all… but then when you look back, it's like another life, not the one you lived… sometimes you tell yourself you're just a little piece of life, and you're alive, that's all, basta… no big deal… but if you're after "The Truth," or God forbid, the "Purpose of It All," that's like trying to learn truth and purpose by staring at a plum tree… it takes so long for me to get it together… mornings, you wake up in chaos and when you go to bed again at night, chaos again… like back before the Creation… What I mean is… let me try to say this more clearly… the thing is, there are so many cripples around since the war. What's gonna happen to them?

UNBESCHWERT: Why, of course, they'll be fed, and clothed. They'll be supported by society and they'll live just as happily as everyone else.

HINKEMANN: What if, for instance, a guy had no arms?

UNBESCHWERT: He'll get artificial arms. And if he's willing and able to work, he'll be assigned a light job.

HINKEMANN: And if a guy has no legs?

UNBESCHWERT: Society will help him, same as the guy with no arms.

HINKEMANN: And what if a guy is sick in the soul?

UNBESCHWERT: (*Robust, unsentimental*) He'll be put in an asylum, but not the kind where the orderlies think they're dealing with animals. The sick will be treated with love, they'll be treated well, they'll be treated like human beings.

HINKEMANN: I wasn't thinking of those that are sick in the head or the brain... I mean the kind that are healthy, but sick somehow in the soul.

UNBESCHWERT: There's no such thing! Healthy body, healthy soul. That's just good common sense. Or if a man's sick in the brain then he belongs in an asylum.

HINKEMANN: Another question then. What about a guy who... for instance... who... was in the war (*Gulping*) and got... for instance... got his... got his balls blown off... what... what would become of him in the new society?

(Peter Immergleich snickers quietly.)

UNBESCHWERT: (*Wiping the sweat off his brow with a hand-kerchief*) You ask the darndest questions! They give me the shivers... It's nothing to laugh about, Comrade Immergleich. Such a thing could happen.

KNATSCH: Makes you want to cry, not laugh!

SINGEGOTT: I'd say the heavenly light would shine right down on a man like that, out of merciful love.

UNBESCHWERT: Yes, well, to try and answer your question... to answer your question... as far as I know, scientific materialism has never touched upon this particular problem... Oh, wait, what a fool I am! Hahaha! Of course, now I've got it. There'll be no wars in the new society. Reason won't permit it! It's so simple.

HINKEMANN: Not that simple after all. Say the new society has been created, there might still be such cripples around from before. How are they supposed to find happiness? Or else, it could happen, you know, at a machine or someplace else... a guy might get his... he could get his... you know... caught... How's a guy like that supposed to find happiness?

UNBESCHWERT: Another one of your questions. A damn twisted one too.

KNATSCH: Nitpicking! People are happiest when they don't think about that sort of thing. And we workers in the revolutionary struggle, we've got no time to waste on trifles. Alright, so if it does happen by chance, that's our sacrifice. The proletariat has a right to sacrifices.

HINKEMANN: I agree with you. But we can still talk about such things. It's a part of life. And since we are talking about it, let me answer my own question. I'd like to tell you a story... There was once a man. Not a remarkable man. Not a leader. A man of the people. A worker. He was a friend of mine. I like him a lot. At twenty he got married. Met his wife at the plant. They were a handsome couple. It always made me happy to see the two of them. She a delicate little woman, he a man of steel... a lot stronger even than me... and so proud of his strength... . And when the Great War broke out, the "Hero's" War, they drafted him. Into the infantry. He had no kids. Salary too small for a family. Back home, he really loved his wife, you understand. But it was only out there in the battlefield that he thought he saw her in her true light. So good... so kind... his heart glowed every time he thought about his wife. And he did constantly. And then all of a sudden he had this overwhelming desire: A child! No, two... three... four... five kids! Boys! Girls! What a perfect mother his wife was gonna make! He forgot what it's really like in a worker's family with lots of kids. What did he know of life back then, of nature, of the earth, of the forest! All week long we were slaves to the job. And Sundays, we went to the silent flics to watch a lot of pretty lies on screen. The one about the wealthy gentleman who picked the poor girl out of the gutter, and other nonsense like that. My God, what kind of life did we lead! A fantasy life, not a real one! A machine-made life! ... Then, in combat, once, he got wounded. A one-way ticket home, he thought, and he was very happy. He hadn't yet had any home-leave. When he woke up in the hospital he touched his body. He felt a bandage 'round his middle. So that's it, he thought, a stomach wound. Then he heard a voice from the next bed: "Our eunuch is up! Won't he be surprised!" They can't be talking about me, he thought. Why do they say eunuch? He lay stiff and quiet. Shut his eyes again. That's how it is, you shut your eyes when there's something you don't want to see. He didn't sleep all night. The next morning he found out. At first he shrieked for days on end... like a wounded animal... until he noticed suddenly that his shriek was a thin falsetto. Then he stopped. He wanted to think about his wife. But whenever he tried, he shut his eyes right away, and lay there, stiff as a board, like he was unconscious, like he'd done the first day after the operation... He wanted to hang himself. He didn't have the courage... . He went home. First thing, he came to see me. We were good friends. What should he do? How should he tell his wife? I felt sick inside. So you're one of those now, I thought, one of those... I pitied him, but I'll admit I also found him just a little bit repulsive. When I thought about it, his situation seemed ridiculous. I couldn't give him any advice. I watched him. I watched his wife. I saw how he suffered. But what do we really see of each other? You sit there and I sit here. How do I see you? I see a few gestures, I hear a few words. That's all... that's nothing, we don't see a thing... we know nothing of each other...

(Growing ever more agitated)

He must've gone through hell! Through hell, I tell you, through hell! A miracle he could go on living at all... But then one day he came to see me, and I noticed right away, there was a strange new beauty about him. You don't say about a man that he looks more beautiful, but it was true. You had the feeling he'd become a different person, somebody rich and happy. And why? Because his wife did not detest him, his wife did not hate him, his wife did not laugh at him... No way to get around it, she was a healthy woman and he a sick man... But he knew that she loved him despite everything. That woman simply... how should I put it... you wouldn't think it was possible... that woman... loved his soul.

(Silence.)

*(Enter **PAUL GROSSHAHN** who is noticeably drunk.)*

GROSSHAHN: Evening, everybody! Cat got your tongue!? Music! Music!

(GROSSHAHN *drops a coin in the jukebox. The record fiddles, squalls, rattles and drums a military march. PAUL GROSS-HAHN sits down at* HINKEMANN'*s table.*)

GROSSHAHN: Evening, Eugene!

HINKEMANN: Evening.

GROSSHAHN: (*With a heavy drunken voice*) It's a wonder your Grete ever let you go… you… haha… you German hero you!

HINKEMANN: What are you talking about?

GROSSHAHN: You incarnation of German muscle! Haha! Devours living rats and mice! Haha!

HINKEMANN: Where'd you find out, Paul? Keep your voice down… It's so awful what I do. I can't even put it into words. It's worse than if I had to bite myself in the throat. There are things that should never be done. And here I am doing this… how can I make you understand? You see, Grete isn't well! The pension's just not enough. It's not like it's my fault that I haven't got a job. But you know what women are like, they can easily get to hate a husband, if they're missing the essentials. I won't let it come to that. That's why… You won't tell Grete, promise me you won't.

GROSSHAHN: I promise.

HINKEMANN: Grete's so sensitive. If she heard I swallowed rat blood and mouse blood… I don't know… I think it'd make her sick…

GROSSHAHN: (*Suddenly, in unabashed indignation*) Hey... that business about being the strongest man, the German hero, that's outright swindle. If the police ever found out!

HINKEMANN: (*Suspiciously*) What do you mean?

GROSSHAHN: What do I mean? The thing is, you see, the reason I can promise not to tell... Grete already saw you.

HINKEMANN: (*Agitated*) What did she say? Did she cry? ... Tell me... tell me...

GROSSHAHN: Cry? The hell she cried! She laughed! First she threw up... then she laughed...

HINKEMANN: (*Overcome*) First she threw up... then she... she laughed... laughed... she laughed... hahaha... she laughed...

GROSSHAHN: Why not laugh at a guy who... who... haha... pretends to be the strongest man and ain't really a man at all! He ain't a man at all!

HINKEMANN: (*Very quietly again*) Who... who told you?

GROSSHAHN: Who? Grete.

HINKEMANN: When?

GROSSHAHN: Out at the amusement park.

HINKEMANN: How'd the two of you get out there?

GROSSHAHN: What's she supposed to live like a nun or

something? How we got there? What kind of question is that! You ought to be ashamed of yourself!

HINKEMANN: Ashamed? I ought to be ashamed?

GROSSHAHN: Who else? Me maybe? Or Grete? Who gives you the right to hold onto your wife? Besides, it's legal grounds for a divorce! Even for the Catholic Church, and they don't recognize any other reasons.

HINKEMANN: (*Quietly*) You see, now there's something I completely forgot. First my country sends me off to war, gets me crippled. And then because I'm crippled, my wife has legal grounds for divorce. I forgot that the world works like that... So what are you plans... about Grete, I mean?

GROSSHAHN: What business is that of yours?

HINKEMANN: You're right. It's really none of my business. Seeing as I'm legal grounds for divorce... But let's just say Grete was some woman you knew and I was your friend. What are you plans?

GROSSHAHN: (*Leering*) My pleasure.

HINKEMANN: Grete's no whore... I mean... alright... we can take that for granted, it's bound to happen anyway... the husband sets her free. Are you going to marry her?

GROSSHAHN: She doesn't want that. She just wants a little pleasure, that's all. Between me'n you. And if she can't get enough from me, why I'll let her out on the streets... maybe make a little for my trouble.

HINKEMANN: (*Quietly, but in a restrained rage*) You... pig!

GROSSHAHN: So... so... I'm a pig, am I! You don't really think I'd let her hit the street! And you call me your friend!

KNATSCH: What's with you two? What are you fighting here in the bar for? Go battle it out with your womenfolk at home.

GROSSHAHN: We're not fighting, we're laughing, that's all.

KNATSCH: Then I'd sure like to hear you fight.

GROSSHAHN: You see, we were just over at the amusement park and...

HINKEMANN: (*Grabs GROSSHAHN by the arm*) Paul... not for my sake, for Grete's, shut up!

GROSSHAHN: ... and we saw the strongest man in the world. Fit as a bear! He devoured live rats and mice, ate 'em alive, he did...

KNATSCH: Only Europeans could take pleasure in that sort of thing!

GROSSHAHN: So I'm givin' this guy the once over, and what do you know, for cryin' out loud: the strongest man in the world is a pal o' mine, guy got both his balls blown off. Bam! Bam! ... strongest man 'n a worl' ain' a man at all, he's a eunuch!

(*Everyone, including SINGEGOTT, and even UNBESCHWERT howl with laughter.*)

(The laughter stings HINKEMANN's flaming, wounded eyes.)

GROSSHAHN: *(Yelling amidst the laughter of the others)* And ya know who it was...

(At that instant HINKEMANN jumps up from his chair. He stands right in the spotlight.)

HINKEMANN: *(Halting and slow at first, and despite the pain, still searching for the right words, finally with the force of great simplicity)* It was Eugene Hinkemann! Go on, laugh it up! Everybody, laugh! Just like that woman laughed! Go on, laugh it up, I said! Best show in town! Looky here! A real live eunuch on display! Want to hear 'im sing?
(Sings in a falsetto) "Why bother crying, when breaking up's a brand new break... ?" Don't I sing just as sweet as a blind canary?... You fatheads! What do you know of the sufferings of a fellow creature? How different you'd have to be to really build a new society! Go battle it out with the bourgeois and swallow his gall, his self-righteousness, his heartlessness! Each of you hates the other because he belongs to a different sect, because he swears by some other party program! Not one of you trusts the others. Not one of you trusts himself! There's not a single honest action that won't suffocate in all your petty bickering and betrayals. You've got your phrases, fine phrases, holy phrases, all about eternal happiness. Those words are fine for the healthy! Don't you see where all your bounty stops... There are people that no state and no society, no family and no community will ever help. Where your salvation ends, our need begins...
Here stands a man alone.
Here looms an abyss, call it: No consolation.
Here floats a heaven, call it: No happiness.
Here grows a forest, call it: Scorn and ridicule.

Here flows an ocean, call it: Pathetic.
Here darkness chokes, call it: No love.
And not a soul around to help...

(A few moments of silence. HINKEMANN stumbles to the door.)

KNATSCH: Where are you going?

HINKEMANN: (*As though a mask had swallowed up his voice*) She laughed, she laughed at me!

(The rest of the scene moves quickly. The stage is dimly lit. The individual figures are recognizable only by their silhouettes.)

UNBESCHWERT: (*Dashes to the door*) Hinkemann! Hinkemann! ... Gone!... If only we'd known... This damn world of ours is to blame!

SINGEGOTT: (*Hysterically*) I blew out the heavenly light! I jeered at a man on the cross!

GROSSHAHN: (*In a whimpering stammer*) S... somebody's gotta h... help...

IMMERGLEICH: Just so you know it, Grosshahn... you're a filthy son of a bitch!

KNATSCH: (*Jumping up*) It's all so simple! Nothing is simple!.. Check please, Frau Heinrich!

Curtain.

ACT THREE

Scene One

A street in the West End. Dusk. As the curtain rises we see HINKEMANN in the foreground hugging a lamppost. A little boy walks up to HINKEMANN.

BOY: Sister thirteen.

HINKEMANN: (*Preoccupied*) I don't doubt it.

BOY: Sister pretty. Sister only thirteen.

HINKEMANN: (*Mechanically*) Are you hungry?

BOY: Sister has extra room. Sister only thirteen.

(HINKEMANN *buys waffles from a woman street vendor. Gives them to the boy.*)

HINKEMANN: So your sister's only thirteen... how old are you?

BOY: Seven... (*Starts eating the waffles*) Thanks a lot... But it's no use talking to you... hell, you're so dumb... you don't get it...

(The LITTLE BOY runs away. The streetlamp lights up. The street is crowded.)
(The IMPRESARIO walks by in tails and a top hat, just a little tipsy.)

IMPRESARIO: Well, I'll be... if it isn't... it's Hinkemann. How ya doin', Hinkemann! But you shouldn't be parading around in public. Rarities must not desecrate themselves. Why a man of qualities ought not to be savored for free. An act like yours! With that act we'll conquer Europe! We'll rediscover America all over again... What are you gaping at? Standing around like a ghost...

HINKEMANN: Mr. Impresario, Sir... murder's back in fashion! Look around you, Sir! Look around! I can see through it all now, Sir. They've blinded me! The glaring light! Nighttime! Let there be night! Let there be night!

IMPRESARIO: What'd you just stumble out of a bar or somethin'? That rot gut packs a punch! Watch it, Hinkemann! Lemme give you some good advice! Better a bottle of wine than five jugs of rotgut. Fine business for the proprietor, gin mill like that, but a damn bad deal for the customers.

HINKEMANN: No Sir, Mr. Impresario, the visit paid off. They blinded me. Now I can see! I can see it all through and through! Right down to the bones. Down to the bare bones. I see what people are like! I see this time of ours! Yes Sir, war's back again! People kill each other and break out laughing! KILL AND DIE LAUGHING!

IMPRESARIO: Fine, so you're a clairvoyant now. Then you ought to be able to see that nobody gives a hoot about war anymore. Atrocity tales ain't worth a dime nowadays. No, that's definitely out! Culture's on the upswing in Europe today! Hundred percent profit-making venture! Yes, culture's really moving again. Strutting and singing and showing its stuff! Open your eyes, my boy! All you need is an act! A routine! That's the key to our time! Any act'll do! Champion boxer! Demagogue! Black marketer! Numbers racketeer! Long distance runner! Shylock! Shimmy dancer! Minister of something or other! Bloodthirsty patriot! Champagne manufacturer! Soothsayer! Master tenor! People's avenger! Jew hater! Business is better than ever! You've got to flow with the tide! A little honest guile will bring a handsome profit nowadays. Necessary dose of ethics thrown in at no extra charge. Haha! Tickled a Negress in Hamburg once... race, I tell you! Until tomorrow then, I'll be expecting you right on time, my boy!

HINKEMANN: Sorry, Sir, that's all over with.

IMPRESARIO: He's joking! That's a good one. Now that you're just getting into the swing of it! Now that you can do it to music!
(*Singing*)
"Faithfully guided!"... Down the hatch! The first bite! ...
(*Singing*)
"Drawn by the heart!" ... Ladies and gentlemen, the man drinks blood!
(*Singing*)
"Where the ble... ess... ing of love leads tonight." Who'll go it again? Who dares!... Homunculus, go sleep it off!

HINKEMANN: No more, Sir... just can't do it anymore... I still have your advance. All that's gotta be settled. Let no one say I cheated strangers. We'll have to work that out.

IMPRESARIO: What? You mean you're serious about this nonsense? Nay, my fine friend, a joke is a joke and serious is serious. Who signed a contract for the whole season? You or I?
(*Brutally*) Listen up, Mister, I'll get the police to drag you

to work. The contract, Mister: Foundation of our great society. The state stands behind me, Mister. Nothing will come of this! Either you show up tomorrow on time or you'll show up under police escort.

(*Changing his tone*) No shenanigans now, Hinkemann, you know I mean the best for you. We wouldn't want to see you land in the clinker.

HINKEMANN: You see, Mr. Impresario, Sir, here you are talking about prison. Those rats and mice whose throats I bit, they sat in prison long before their execution. And some people are free and still behind bars, and haven't done anything wrong... just like those animals in the cage. It's a barred window and it cuts off the light. Invisible walls... life smashes against them and dies. There are chains that grow under the skin. You can't scare me, Mr. Impresario. And besides...

(*Screaming, full of hate*) ... you... you're the devil himself! The devil! You feed blood to the masses! You rob them of their shame! I... I... oh I'd like to... but there'll be others after me, they'll take care of the likes of you, they will! And you know something, there's a woman who laughed at Homunculus. And that woman is my wife.

(*Bitterly*) She laughed the longest, that woman did, and now she's gonna cry. But... you see, we've got wax in our ears, wax kneaded by laughter and scorn.

IMPRESARIO: (*Enraged*) Will somebody get a load o' this! Guy stammers around like he can't even get three syllables out, and now all of a sudden, he's turned into a flaming radical. What I do? What I am? I'll tell you what I am, I'm an upstanding businessman, a loyal servant of the state...

(*Jovially*) Can't take you seriously, Hinkemann. You're drunk. We'll talk it all over tomorrow. You'd better get your act together, son! Or you'll get trampled under. Why a man with your qualities! See you tomorrow, you hit of the season, you! Till tomorrow then!

(The impresario walks off.)

HINKEMANN: (*Alone*) Tomorrow... the way he says it... tomorrow... like there had to be a tomorrow. Oh I see it! I see it all! Oh, the light! Oh, my eyes!... my eyes...

(Hinkemann collapses. The following must be performed like Hinkemann's nightmare.)

(All the figures seem to close in upon him, and then to fade again, dissolving in the dark.)

(From all sides numerous one-armed and one-legged war invalids enter, grinding organs. They gather in a circle and sing the following soldier's song in a matter-of-fact manner.)

INVALIDS: A bullet flew at me from behind
This faithful breast shot through,
And here I lie 'neath foreign fields,
My dear, thinking, oh thinking of you...

(Suddenly they all stop.)

INVALIDS: (*One after the other call out*) Company halt!

(No one makes a move.)

INVALIDS: (*All cry out in unison*) Company halt!"

(A few seconds of silence. Since no one retreats, all start up again, as if on command, singing and playing, marching at

each other. As though fired with a revolutionary zeal, like they were on the verge of storming some bastion of reactionary order, they sing this song, grinding their organs fanatically all the while.)

INVALIDS: (*Singing in unison*)
 Down with the dogs, down with the dogs,
 Down with the dirty, reactionary dogs!

(The organs rattle against each other, causing a terrible racket. Having retreated from the onslaught, the men once again march at each other.)

(A few policemen come running. We hear the cries of the police.)

POLICE: Law and Order!...In the name of the Law!...Soldiers of our country!

(Sudden silence follows, as though a familiar sound demanding silence had impressed itself on the ears of the invalids. They do a military about-face and march off in strict formation in various directions, but always keeping to the same radius. Meanwhile they play their organs and sing in a soldierly fashion.)

INVALIDS: We'll beat the French to victory...

(NEWSBOYS run across the stage.)

FIRST NEWSBOY: Extra! Extra! Great sensation! Gala opening at the Victoria Bar. Naked dancers! Jazz band! French champagne! American mixer!

SECOND NEWSBOY: Evening edition! Latest sensation! Pogrom in Galicia! Synagogues on fire! Thousands burnt alive!

A VOICE: Bravo! Round up the Jews! Send 'em all to Galicia!

THIRD NEWSBOY: Tria Trei! Vamp of the silver screen! Tria Trei stars in thriller: "Sex Killer and her Forty Victims" Riveting! Brutal! Red hot!

FOURTH NEWSBOY: Epidemic in Finland! Mothers drown children! Sensational eyewitness report! Revolt of the Proletariat! German troops sent in to preserve law and order! A hundred tanks on the road to Finland!

FIFTH NEWSBOY: New spirit spreads through the Heartland! Rebirth of morality! Christ's message in our time! Stirring screen drama: "The Passion of Our Lord Jesus Christ" starring the great Glin Glanda as the savior. A million-dollar production! And as an extra added attraction, the Carpenter-Dempsey heavyweight match!

SIXTH NEWSBOY: The invention of the 20th-century! Levicite! Technical wonder! Miraculous poison gas! Single bomber squadron capacity to obliterate metropolis, people, plants, animals and all. Inventor honored worldwide, named to learned academies! Knighted by the Pope!

SEVENTH NEWSBOY: The dollar drops! The dollar drops! Birthrate on the rise! Latest government statistics! Welcome news to population experts!

EIGHTH NEWSBOY: Lottery for the poor! Hundred percent dividends! Solution to the social problem! Solution to the social problem!

(Two old Jews walk across the stage.)

FIRST JEW: What's there to tell? They beat us, they tore us out of bed in the middle of the night, they took our wives and daughters... God smote us with suffering.

SECOND JEW: What suffering? We're the chosen people! Which means? Chosen! Chosen to suffer! Some favor God did us!

(*They pass by.*)

LITTLE LOVE MACHINE: He was so nice, so innocent... so I stayed the whole night... I didn't care how much he gave me...

PIMP: I'll give it to you, right in the kisser, next time you give it away just for love...

LITTLE LOVE MACHINE: ... but I'm so sick...

(*They pass by.*)

OLD WAFFLE VENDOR: Don't you defame the New Messiah, Mister! Don't you malign his name! He gives us old workhorses hope again! The dawn is rising. The blessed Kingdom of Zion is near.

CUSTOMER: And he'll take every last penny you've got.

OLD WAFFLE VENDOR: And what of it, Mister, what good is all that worthless paper? Can an old bag of bones like me have it any worse? I'm not afraid of worldly trials and tribulations. I've sipped it all down to the dregs. Oh how my soul thirsts for redemption. I know the Kingdom of Zion is near.

(They pass.)

(A street vendor tries hard-sell techniques on a gentleman wearing a standup collar and a monocle.)

STREET VENDOR: Latest cure for impotence, "Man Alive."

MAN WITH COLLAR: No thanks, I use "Society" brand.

STREET VENDOR: Don't you know they went out of business! Turned out to be a fraud. Candy-coated fraud. Society's the brand name of a shoe polish now.

(They pass.)

CRIES: Some guy out cold! A stroke! Police!

VOICES: That's Homunculus, from the side show! That's what all that rat blood'll do to you. It's no wonder!

COP WITH NIGHTSTICK: One o' them Commie bastards, I bet. Like the Prussian guy ... ha... short trial... gave the fool a gun... made him shoot himself or else we'd've busted his head open for him! And just before he pulled the trigger, made him sing: "Deutschland, Deutschland Über Alles"... Hahaha... pack o' dogs gotta learn who's master again... break their goddamn neck for 'em.

MAN WITH FLAMETHROWER: Never took no prisoners in our division. On command: Alright, double time... step on his toes... make 'im jump... blam, right in the ass... report after, attempted escape...

(Whores come running from all directions.)

FIRST WHORE: Homunculus can stay with me. Bring 'im over to my place. I'll give 'im a drink, make 'im come to, I will...

SECOND WHORE: No, you don't... he's comin' home with me!

THIRD WHORE: He's mine! He's mine!

FOURTH WHORE: Like hell he's yours, you old cow! You ain't even registered, honey! Get lost!

(THIRD and FOURTH WHORES start a fight.)

(Military music thunders from a nearby street. First Fife and drums, then brass with a huge blast.)

OFFICER: Forward march!

CRIES: Soldiers! Soldiers! Hurrah! Hurrah!

(Everyone abandons HINKEMANN and runs away. The street is completely empty. Even the street lamps seem to have grown small and dim, as if in response to the soldiers. The military music fades in the distance. HINKEMANN gets up.)

HINKEMANN: And up there the sky eternal... and the stars still looking down...

(Stage goes dark.)

ACT THREE
Scene Two

Implied setting. Hinkemann's apartment.
Max Knatsch stands waiting at a table.
Hinkemann enters carrying a wrapped-up object in his hand.
His eyes are feverish; his gestures, in contrast to before, are
downright giddy.

KNATSCH: I've been waiting for you, Hinkemann… I wanted
to explain… the reasons… why…

HINKEMANN: Don't bother, neighbor. Reasons are irrele-
vant. Feelings count. You know what I've got here in my
hand?

KNATSCH: How should I…

HINKEMANN: The reason of them all! No reasons. The reason itself! I was walking past a show window, and when
I looked in I didn't know whether to burst out laughing
or crying. I shut my eyes, because I thought, maybe I'm
dreaming. And when I opened them again, there was
this thing still lying there in the window. So I went inside
and I ask them why they put this thing in the window.
'It's a priapus,' the salesman says. And seeing as I don't
follow, he explains how ancient Romans and Greeks
used to pray to it like a God. 'You mean the women?'
I ask. 'No,' he says, 'the men and the women.' 'Is it for
sale?' 'Yes.' 'On the installment plan?' 'Cash only here.'

I apologize and explain that installment buying's all we workers know. I left my watch and bought the god.

(*Hinkemann removes the paper wrapping from a small brass priapus. He stands it on the stove, lights a candle and sets it beside the priapus.*)

KNATSCH: (*Gently urging*) You don't feel well, Hinkemann... you don't look well... you're ill...

HINKEMANN: Could be.

KNATSCH: You know... I think I just might... stay with you, till your wife gets home.

HINKEMANN: Step on a crack, break your mother's back.

KNATSCH: What are you talking about?

HINKEMANN: Just a second! Have you ever really looked at people on the street?

KNATSCH: What kind of crazy questions!

HINKEMANN: Day in day out you walk the streets like you were blind. Then all of a sudden you see. It's awful, Knatsch, the things you see. You see the naked soul. You want to know what the soul looks like? Not like any living thing. One soul's a fat neck, the other's a machine, the third is a cash register, the fourth is an army helmet, the fifth is a nightstick... You ever poked a canary's eyes out?
(*Without waiting for Knatsch's response*) The sins of the mother shall be avenged until the fourth generation. Isn't that what it says... Good night, Knatsch. No

sympathy for the devil... I know, I know... the reason... the reasons...

KNATSCH: Maybe it'd be better if I stayed a while.

HINKEMANN: It's okay, really... it's okay... Grete'll be home any minute now... Back at the bar... that was just the whiskey talking...

KNATSCH: Alright then, Eugene... goodnight.

HINKEMANN: Goodnight, Max... Just one more question. How long have you been married?

KNATSCH: Twenty-three years.

HINKEMANN: You wanted to get a divorce once, didn't you?

KNATSCH: I thought about it. But people get used to each other. And the kids, they're the cement that holds it together.

HINKEMANN: Cement—children... Divorce, that means separation from bed and breakfast, doesn't it?

KNATSCH: I guess.

HINKEMANN: And your wife, she's religious?

KNATSCH: Never missed a mass... What are you gonna do? So, let her go to church, if she gets a kick out of it...
(*At the door*)
Good night, Eugene.

(*Max Knatsch leaves.*)

HINKEMANN: There's no other God but you. How they lie to themselves and cheat themselves, and make as if they're praying to the crucified one. They're praying to you! Every Ave is consecrated to you, every Our Father's a rosary to hide your nakedness, every procession a dance to honor you! You wear no masks, you don't hide behind hypocritical phrases, you are the alpha and the omega, the beginning and the end, you are the truth, you are the one true God of all peoples... You have cast off your faithful servant, Oh Lord, but see, your servant has erected an altar to you... Ha, I think he's laughing! The people laughed at me, but you had no reason. Now you're laughing... too! You have a right to laugh.

(Sound on the stairway.)

HINKEMANN: Grete's coming... it's getting dark and my eyes are going blind...

(Enter Hinkemann's mother.)

HINKEMANN'S MOTHER: Evening.

HINKEMANN: It's you... evening, Mother. What brings you here at this late hour? Since when are you out on the streets after dark? Is it the warm summer night air?... The swallows were flying low today. There's bound to be a storm.

HINKEMANN'S MOTHER: He came back.

HINKEMANN: Who?

HINKEMANN'S MOTHER: Your father.

HINKEMANN: What father?

HINKEMANN'S MOTHER: Your father.

HINKEMANN: Mother, what are you talking about? My father died when I was less than a year old. How many times have you told me that!

HINKEMANN'S MOTHER: I lied to you. He died, that he did. For me he died. You were half a year old. I still suckled you on this same breast, so withered and wasted now. He came home one evening. Drunk. With some tart on his arm. Picked her up off the street, he did. 'Woman,' he yelled, 'go to your parents' house and sleep there tonight. I need young blood in my bed. You give me the chills ever since you birthed that whelp.'... I looked him right in the eye. And all of a sudden, it wasn't my husband standing there before me, it was a wild animal that wanted to hurt me and my child. I grabbed a kitchen knife and held it to his breast... He laughed at me, took his tart and left. He didn't come back that night. Nor the night after. He left me like he'd never known me. I worked the streets then... to earn a mouthful for you. I wasn't ugly in those days. And today...

HINKEMANN: Today?

HINKEMANN'S MOTHER: He came back. Dressed in stolen, tattered, matted rags, his body lousy with bugs. Bloated, sick, shivering, he felt his way up. I recognized him on the spot, soon as I saw him climbing up the stairs. 'What do you want from me after twenty-nine years?' I asked him. 'You won't beat me, will you?' he muttered like a batty old fool. And then: 'I came back to die here.'

HINKEMANN: And what did you say to him, Mother?

HINKEMANN'S MOTHER: I told him to get undressed and climb into bed. That he'd find clean linen in the closet, warm water on the stove, soap in the drawer.

HINKEMANN: So you forgave him, Mother?

HINKEMANN'S MOTHER: (*With a hard tone of voice*) No, and I'll never forgive him. I'll care for him till his dying day. That's my human duty. And when he dies, I'll shut his eyes for him, I'll never let no stranger do that in my place... But when they drive him to the graveyard, then I'll pull down my shades and lock my door and I won't walk behind the coffin.
(*Triumphantly*) Strangers will bury him! That will be my revenge for what he did to me!

HINKEMANN: (*After a pause*) What was the worst of it, Mother? Was it that he drank up his earnings while you went hungry?

HINKEMANN'S MOTHER: No.

HINKEMANN: Was it that he took up with a whore?

HINKEMANN'S MOTHER: No.

HINKEMANN: That he wanted to lie with her in your bed?

HINKEMANN'S MOTHER: No, that wasn't it.

HINKEMANN: I know, Mother: that he laughed at you when your soul cried out?

HINKEMANN'S MOTHER: Yes, Eugene, that was it.

HINKEMANN: Then you're doing the right thing, Mother. I won't see Father, and, like you, I won't walk behind his coffin.

(Silence.)

HINKEMANN'S MOTHER: Eugene... I need a suit for your father.

HINKEMANN: Here's my Sunday suit, Mother, take it.

(Hinkemann takes a suit out of the closet and hands it to his mother.)

HINKEMANN'S MOTHER: It'll fit him for sure... you know, your father was always very particular about his clothes... Grete home?

HINKEMANN: She'll be back soon, Mother... Mother, you carry your misfortune and I carry mine. You can talk about it... but I, I can't tell anyone, I'd be afraid of being laughed at.

HINKEMANN'S MOTHER: To each his own burden, my son. Nothing for nothing in this world. Life's much stronger than us little people, Eugene. I've got to be getting home now. Your father'll be hungry. Good night.

HINKEMANN: Good night, Mother.

(HINKEMANN'S MOTHER leaves.)

HINKEMANN: That was the worst of it: that he laughed at her when her soul cried out. Did you hear that, great God? Are you satisfied? Two more souls sacrificed to you... my father become Milord's whoremonger, my mother your cooing ringdove. Shall we dance for joy? Your wish is our command! I can do anything. Gulp down rat blood for twenty cents admission, dance for the two lost lives. Hahaha!

(HINKEMANN starts swinging his arms and hopping from one leg to the other in front of the priapus, slowly at first, then ever faster to a wild dance rhythm.)

HINKEMANN: Merrily! Merrily! Hoppla! Hoppla! Right this way, ladies and gentlemen! Tickets! Tickets! The more the merrier! Hohoho! Hohoho!

(HINKEMANN sinks down on a footstool.)

(After a while FRÄNZE enters.)

FRÄNZE: Evening. Grete not home?

HINKEMANN: No.

FRÄNZE: You look so sad... the air is sweet on a warm summer night... I'm going dancing... wanna come?

HINKEMANN: For God's sake! Oh, sorry... my mind was somewhere else.

FRÄNZE: Hey, Eugene...

HINKEMANN: Yeah?

FRÄNZE: Eugene...

HINKEMANN: What!

FRÄNZE: You're still the strongest of them all... and the handsomest.

HINKEMANN: So?

FRÄNZE: I was just thinking, you know...

HINKEMANN: What?

FRÄNZE: To look at Grete... she's so moody these days... she's my friend and all... but I don't envy you, I can tell you that much... (*Coming up close to him*)
Hey, Eugene... Eugene, come on! You can tell Grete you had a Party meeting to attend, oh come on, you know what I mean!

HINKEMANN: You mean... you mean we should spend the night together? That's what you're driving at, isn't it? The night air is so warm. On the stairway you trip over frenzied cats. In the park... the air is so sweet...

FRÄNZE: It's so warm out, Eugene, we could sleep on a park bench... come on, Eugene...

(*FRÄNZE cuddles up to HINKEMANN, kisses him.*)

(*HINKEMANN shoves her away and laughs out loud.*)

FRÄNZE: (*In a rage*) You think I'm running after you?

HINKEMANN: You just go run along, little lady. There are loads of men in the park. Tomcats and she-cats, hounds and bitches all over the place. The air is warm.

FRÄNZE: (*Seething*) Next time you'll come begging!

(*FRÄNZE runs out.*)

HINKEMANN: Hahaha! The dead Hinkemann is still a God! There's a naked bronze statue in the marketplace. Like flies they swarm around him!... Step right up, ladies and gentlemen! Be amazed!... And me, a legal grounds for divorce.

(A few seconds silence. GRETE enters.)

GRETE: Evening, Eugene.

HINKEMANN: *(Without looking up)* And the Lord said to Cain: 'Where is Abel, they brother?' And he said: 'I know not; am I my brother's keeper?'

GRETE: It's me, Eugene.

HINKEMANN: And He said: 'What hast thou done? The voice of thy brother's blood crieth out unto Me from the ground.'

GRETE: I brought you some flowers, Eugene... it's our anniversary today...

HINKEMANN: Some people hide behind a mask. They can laugh at you and pretend affection all in the same breath... I thank you, Grete! You're very kind, Grete. The flowers are so colorful. How good the colors make me feel! It was nice, our wedding day... our first night... very nice.

GRETE: That was still during peacetime.

HINKEMANN: Yes, and then came the war. You said, 'I'm so proud of you in that uniform.' And you cried when I went off to war. Did you cry for joy, that I served in the honor guard?

GRETE: What dreams we had then!

HINKEMANN: Dreams, yes, as bright as these flowers. But there's no place for flowers in war. They blossom in some garden, a grenade hits, and that's the end of the flowers. Plants get it, just like animals, and animals just like people. No difference... I was a handsome buck and I lived and never thought about tomorrow. You were always jealous.

GRETE: Yes.

HINKEMANN: (*Hard*) But now you don't need to be jealous any more, now you can... laugh!

GRETE: (*Starts crying*)

HINKEMANN: Come on, laugh it up! You're crying? Don't put on a show for me! Laugh, woman, laugh! You learned how to laugh. You know how to laugh when somebody lays his scarred naked soul in the gutter. Save your tears! Oh yes, I forgot... gotta sing for you first!
(*Sings in a falsetto*)
'Vilja, oh Vilja, du Wandmägdelein.' Why aren't you laughing? (*Exhausted*) I did my little song and dance, didn't I!

GRETE: (*With open palms outstretched and fingers stiff with fear*) The way you look at me... I'm afraid of you...

HINKEMANN: Afraid? Nonsense! How can you be afraid of me, afraid of a guy who isn't even... who isn't even...

GRETE: (*Abruptly, submissively*) No, no, I'm not afraid at all. I love you, how could I be afraid of you?

HINKEMANN: The truth, woman!

GRETE: I want to tell it.

HINKEMANN: I know everything.

GRETE: I was wicked, Eugene.

HINKEMANN: You're not lying?

GRETE: I was bad. I'm a weak woman. It was all just too much for me. I loved you and yet I didn't love you. It was wrong of me. I don't know if you can still love me...

HINKEMANN: How can I blame you for going with Paul? That was your perfect right, if you love him.

GRETE: (*Not comprehending*) ... So you don't love me?

HINKEMANN: Because I love you.

GRETE: (*Not comprehending*) No... no...

HINKEMANN: But you'd better leave quickly, Grete, quickly! ... Or... no... I'll go... I'll make no demands. The furniture's all yours. Goodbye.

GRETE: Eugene! Eugene! My poor dear husband! I sold you out for a few pieces of silver... I treated you like dirt.

HINKEMANN: You!...You!... Woman! Who taught you how to lie these last few weeks? Or was I deaf before? Did I not know who shared these four walls with me? Did nature betray me? I thought it was a butterfly and it turned into a worm! A worm with cheating eyes, just

like a whore, only difference is, the whore does it to survive.
(*Flying into a rage*)
Don't you touch me! Let go of my hands! Maybe my injured body made you sick, but now, woman, now you make me sick! Your hands: toads, filthy, slimy! Your breasts, your ripe round breasts: like rotten mire! Your body, your healthy body, robust, blooming... I don't what to see it anymore! It's withered in bloom. Like a carcass to my eyes!

GRETE: (*On her knees*) Beat me!... beat me!... strike me! Strike me!... I deserve it!

HINKEMANN: And when you stood there at the side show and heard how your husband put himself on display like an animal... how your husband bit the throats of innocent little creatures... to earn a buck for you! Bit the throats of living creatures! There you stood with your lover boy right in front of the stage, and you... laughed! You laughed!

GRETE: That's not true... by God, I swear, it isn't true!

HINKEMANN: I can't speak another word with you. You lie, not like a human being. You lie like a devil. Goodbye!

(*HINKEMANN turns to leave.*)

GRETE: Say it, Eugene, say it... only stay with me... you can blame me for everything... yes, I laughed at the side show... I laughed like this... hahahaha!

HINKEMANN: And for that you've got to die, woman. Not because you went with another man—that was your right...

not because you lied to me—you took the liberty... you're going to die because you laughed at me! A mother can strangle her child and no one has the right to say she did wrong. But if after strangling that child, she snickers at the swollen tongue hanging from its throat... then let her suffer the torments of hell till the end of time! I'm being merciful with you, woman. I won't let you suffer for eternity... why do you kneel down before me! Kneel before him who is your God. Pray to him!..Pray!

(HINKEMANN drags GRETE before the priapus. His breathing has become a groaning.)

HINKEMANN: (*After a few seconds*) Why... why look at me like that? ... Your eyes?... I swear I'm not human if there's lying in that look!... I know those eyes!... I saw them in the factory... I saw them in the army... I saw them from my hospital bed... I saw those eyes in prison. The same eyes. Eyes of the tormented, the beaten, the tortured, the martyred creature... Oh, Gretchen, I thought you were so much richer than me, and here you are, just as poor, just as helpless... if that's the way it is... if that's really the way it is... then you and I, we're brother and sister. I'm you and you're me... and God, what will become of us?

GRETE: I'll never leave you, never.

HINKEMANN: That's not the point, Grete. All that's behind us now. What does it matter to us? What difference does it make if you go with another man? What difference if you lie to me? If you laugh at me? It won't do you any good. And even if you went around in silken finery and lived in a spacious villa and never stopped laughing—it wouldn't make a bit of difference, you'd still be as poor a creature as me. I see it now... Go, Grete,... leave me alone...

GRETE: Now you want me to leave you?

HINKEMANN: From now on and forever, Grete, you've got to leave me alone. I've got to leave you alone.

GRETE: What'll happen to us?

HINKEMANN: Once, six weeks ago, I was feeling awful. Hunger made my mouth water whenever I saw someone eating! Such a strange sensation, GRETE, I'd be walking through the playgrounds and parks in the rich neighborhoods and I'd see a little boy biting away at a great big sandwich! I was so envious! And suddenly the hunger didn't hurt anymore! And it enraged me—that child chewing on his sandwich! And I could almost have become a murderer, just to stop seeing that little boy chewing!

GRETE: Eugene, what does it all mean? I don't understand any of it.

HINKEMANN: I've become ridiculous and it was my own fault. When the mass-murderers of this world, the statesmen and generals lit that fuse, I should have done something then, but I didn't. I'm ridiculous now like the time we live in, sad and ridiculous as our time. Our time has no soul. And I have no sex. Is there any difference? Let's each of us go our own way, you yours and me mine.

GRETE: Eugene, what are you saying?

HINKEMANN: That I don't know how long I'll be able to live with it, all that I've seen and understood. Nature is stronger than reason. Reason's nothing but an instrument of self deception.

GRETE: And what about me?

HINKEMANN: You're healthy. A sick man has no place on this earth, the way things are… everyone's worth as much as he's good for. If he's healthy, he's got a healthy soul. That's just good common sense. If he's sick in the brain, he belongs in an insane asylum. That's not really true, but it isn't false either. A sick man's good for nothing, he's crippled in the blood. His soul, it's like the broken wing of a lark, like an eagle in the zoo, whose tendons have been clipped… take care, Grete, I wish you well.

GRETE: What are you doing… what are you doing?… You can't leave me alone?…

HINKEMANN: Not because of my sickness… not because of my disfigured body… I've been walking the streets… I didn't see any people there… only masks, hideous masks… I came home and I saw masks and misery… the senseless, unending misery of blind creatures… I haven't got the strength to go on. No more strength to fight, no more strength to dream. He who has no strength to dream, has no strength to live. That shot was a fruit from the tree of knowledge. What I see is what I know, and what I now is nothing but suffering. Some people live through the pain and still want to go on… I don't want to go on.

GRETE: You want to kill yourself!… Eugene… Eugene… I didn't laugh at all. Listen to me! I'm telling you, I… did… not… laugh. Eugene. I want to stay with you. Forever and ever! Everything's gonna be alright again. The two of us together. We won't freeze, you'n me, me'n you…

HINKEMANN: You didn't laugh… Look at me, Grete… I believe you, Grete… O, Grete. (*He kisses her tenderly*) Everything's gonna be alright again… me'n you, you'n me.

GRETE: (*Hugging him*) Summer will come, peace in the trees. Stars will wander arm in arm…

HINKEMANN: (*Loosening himself from her embrace*) Autumn will come, to wither the leaves, Stars… and hatred!… and fist against fist!

GRETE: (*Screaming*) Eugene!

HINKEMANN: (*Wearily*) I know too much.

GRETE: (*Weeping like a helpless child*) Don't leave me alone… I'll go crazy in the dark… I'll hurt myself… I'll fall. I feel so sore all over… It hurts! It hurts! Oh… oh… I'm so scared of life! I can't! Alone! Alone in life! Alone in a forest full of wild animals! Nobody's kind nowadays. Everyone gnaws at your heart… Don't leave me alone!! Don't leave me!! God decreed my fate. I belong with you.

HINKEMANN: An act against nature cannot be an act of God. Try, Grete, try… fight it… fight for a new world… for our world…

GRETE: (*With shoulders trembling*) Even if I… even if I wanted to… I couldn't anymore… I haven't got the nerve, I'm broken.
(*Desperate*) My God, I just can't anymore. We're tangled in a web. The spider keeps watch and she won't let us out. She's woven us into her web. I can hardly still hold up my head. I don't understand this life anymore… Oh save us from evil, my Lord, Jesus Christ…

(She leaves with heavy steps.)

HINKEMANN: (*Alone*) Where is the beginning and where the end? Who can tell in a spider web?

(HINKEMANN grabs the priapus and flings it into the oven.)
You two-faced God! You pathetic sham!...

(After a pause)

If this is the way things are, who among us has the right to pass judgment on another? We're all damned to judge ourselves... Redemption! Redemption! On every street corner all over the world they're crying for redemption! The Frenchman who made a cripple of me, the black man who made a cripple of me, maybe right now he's pleading for redemption... Who knows if he's still alive? And what sort of life does he live?... Is he blind, is he missing an arm, his legs? He hurt me and somebody else hurt him... But who was it hurt us all?... One spirit unites us, one body... And there are those that don't see it. And there are those who've forgotten it. They suffered in war and hated their superiors and they obeyed and they killed!... All forgotten now... They'll suffer again and hate their superiors again and again they'll... obey and again... they'll kill! That's the way people are, and could be different if they wanted to. But they don't want to be different. They fling stones at the spirit, and jeer at it, they mutilate life and crucify it... again and again and again. How senseless! They make themselves poor and could be so rich, and they don't need any heavenly savior to help... Blinded! As if they had to go on like that in the blind whirlwind of the millennia! Couldn't do it any other way. Simply couldn't.

Like ships drawn by the maelstrom and forced to smash
against each other...

(*Outside a hubbub of voices. The door is flung open.*)
(*A crowd storms in, MAX KNATSCH at the lead.*)

KNATSCH: In the yard... in the yard... in the yard... your wife...
she jumped... don't look... don't look... it's so... awful...

(*People carry in GRETE's body wrapped in a blanket.*)

HINKEMANN: (*With a blank stare and mechanical gestures*)
Leave me alone, all of you, leave me alone... leave me
alone with my wife...
(*Pleading*)
... I beg you all.

(*They leave the room.*)

HINKEMANN: She was healthy and she tore her way through
the web. And here I am still standing here, colossal and
ridiculous... And like me, other men will stand there,
each in his own time, asking: Why me? Why did it have
to be me?... It's all so random. He gets hit and he gets
hit. And not him and not him... What do we know?...
Where do we come from?... Where are we headed?...
Every day could bring paradise, and every night anni-
hilation.

The curtain falls.

About Ernst Toller:

ERNST TOLLER was a playwright, born in the Province of Posen in 1893, then part of Prussia, today under Polish dominion. Upon hearing of the outbreak of World War I in 1914, Ernst Toller, who had been studying law in Grenoble, rushed home to enlist in the Kaiser's army. But after witnessing the horrors of war firsthand, getting seriously wounded, and suffering a complete physical and psychological collapse, he was disabused of his youthful nationalist political leanings and embraced revolutionary change. In 1919 he joined the leadership of the short-lived Bavarian Soviet Republic in Munich, serving six days as its president, before being captured, tried for treason, and sentenced to five years in prison.

Toller applied the imposed "leisure" of his incarceration in the German prison Niederschönenfeld, 1921-1922, to the completion of several of his best known plays, including *Hinkemann*, establishing his reputation as one of the foremost young German dramatists at a time when Bertolt Brecht was still a virtual unknown. It was, however, only following his release from prison in 1925 that he got to see his plays performed. Conceived in the German theatrical tradition of Jakob Michael Reinhold Lenz's *Die Soldaten* (The Soldiers) and Georg Büchner's *Woyzeck*, Toller's devastating tragedy *Hinkemann* is a painfully poetic plaidoyer for the overlooked vision and voice of the victim.

Given his notoriety, his Jewish ancestry, political posi-
tion, and avant-garde artistic stance made him an immedi-
ate high profile persona non grata in 1933 when the Nazis
came to power. Toller fled to London, went on a lecture tour
to the U.S. in 1936, and tried to make a go of it in Los Ange-
les, where he took an unsuccessful stab at screenwriting.
Moving to New York City, he joined a group of like-minded
literary émigrés, including Klaus and Erika Mann, the son
and daughter of Thomas Mann, both writers in their own
right. Though two of his plays were staged in English, they
were not well received. Dispirited, despondent upon learn-
ing that his brother and sister had been sent to a concen-
tration camp, and convinced that the world as he knew it
had succumbed to the forces of darkness, Toller was found
dead by hanging, a presumed suicide, in Manhattan in his
room at the Hotel Mayflower on May 22, 1939.

Picture: National Library of Israel, Schwadron collection

About Peter Wortsman:

PETER WORTSMAN is the author of two stage plays, *Burning Words*, premiered in 2006 by the Hampshire Shakespeare Company at the Northampton Center for the Arts, MA., and in 2014 in German translation by the ensemble of the Kulturhaus Osterfeld, in Pforzheim, Germany; and *The Tattooed Man Tells All,* premiered by the Silverthorne Theater in Greenfield, MA, in 2018. He is the author of three books of short fiction, *A Modern Way To Die* (1991), *Footprints in Wet Cement* (2017), and *Stimme und Atem/Out of the Breath, Out of Mind*, a bilingual German-English collection, forthcoming in 2019; a travel memoir, *Ghost Dance in Berlin, A Rhapsody in Gray* (2013); a novel, *Cold Earth Wanderers* (2014); and a work of nonfiction, *The Caring Heirs of Dr. Samuel Bard,* forthcoming in 2019. His critically acclaimed translations from German into English include *Posthumous Papers of a Living Author,* by Robert Musil, now in its third edition (1988, 2005, 2009); and *Tales of the German Imagination, From the Brothers Grimm to Ingeborg Bachmann* (2013), an anthology which he also edited and annotated; and *Konundrum. Selected Prose of Franz Kafka* (2016). Recipient of a 2014 Independent Publishers Book Award (IPPY), he was a fellow of the Fulbright Foundation (1973), the Thomas J. Watson Foundation (1974), and a Holtzbrinck Fellow at the American Academy in Berlin (2010).

Picture: Ricky Owens

Berlinica presents

Upcoming in 2019
New in 2018

Harold L. Poor

KURT TUCHOLSKY

THE SHORT, FAT BERLINER WHO TRIED TO
STOP A CATASTROPHE WITH A TYPEWRITER

Softcover, 280 pp, 6 x 9"
ca 20 bw pictures, $24.95
ISBN: 978-1-935902-47-8
Release: Winter 2018

**New Edition of: Kurt Tucholsky and
The Ordeal of Germany 1914 – 1835**

Donna Swarthout (ed)
A PLACE THEY CALLED HOME
RECLAIMING CITIZENSHIP. STORIES OF A NEW JEWISH RETURN TO GERMANY

English Edition, Hardcover
208 pp, 6" x 9"
12 pictures, List price $ 19,95
ISBN: 978-1-935902-65-2
Release: Winter 2018

Kurt Tucholsky
HEREAFTER
WE WERE SITTING ON THE CLOUD, DANGLING OUR LEGS
TRANSLATED BY CINDY OPITZ

Hardcover, 96pp., 5 x 8"
25 color pictures, $12.95
ISBN: 978-1-935902-89-8
Release: Winter 2018

"Wonderful and touching stories about the afterlive and beyond"

Kurt Tucholsky
GERMANY? GERMANY!
SATIRICAL WRITINGS
TRANSLATED BY HARRY ZOHN
Preface by Ralph Blumenthal

Softcover, 200 pp., 5 pictures, $14.95
ISBN: 978-1-935902-38-6

"He was one of the Weimar era's most acid, incisive satirists."

Kurt Tucholsky

BERLIN! BERLIN!

DISPATCHES FROM THE WEIMAR REPUBLIC

Preface by Anne Nelson
Introduction by Ian King

Softcover, 198 pp., 41 pictures, $13.95
ISBN: 978-1-935902-23-2

". . . the most brilliant, prolific, and witty cultural journalist of his time"

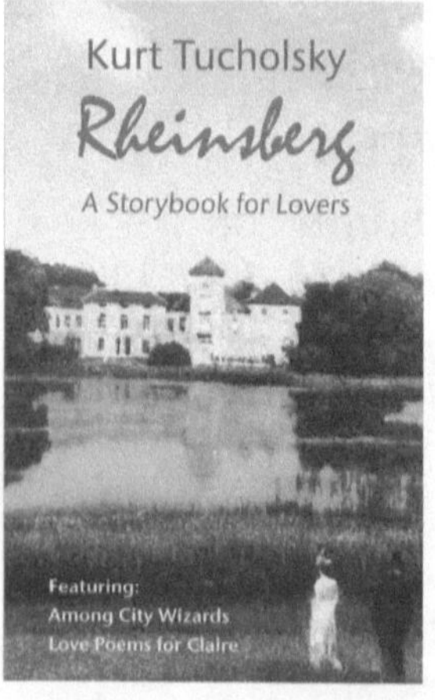

Kurt Tucholsky

RHEINSBERG

A STORYBOOK FOR LOVERS
AMONG CITY WIZARDS / POEMS

Translated by Cindy Opitz
Afterword by Peter Boethig

Hardcover, 5" x 8", 96 pp.
35 Pictures, $ 14.00
ISBN: 978-1-935902-25-6

"Intense wit, charm, and verve!"

Kurt Tucholsky

PRAYER AFTER THE SLAUGHTER

POEMS FROM WORLD WAR I

Bilingual Edition, translated by Peter Appelbaum and James Scott

Softcover, 116 pp., 6 pictures, $12.95, ISBN: 978-1-935902-28-7

"He heaped scorn on the reactionary institutions of the old regime"

Andreas Nachama
Julius Schoeps
Hermann Simon

JEWS IN BERLIN

Preface by Carol Kahn-Strauss

Softcover, 314 pp., $25.95
376 pictures,
ISBN: 978-1-935902-60-7

"... a captivating read that promises a wealth of enjoyment ..."

Andreas Austilat

MARK TWAIN IN BERLIN

NEWLY DISCOVERED STORIES & AN ACCOUNT OF TWAIN'S BERLIN ADVENTURES
Preface by Lewis Lapham

Softcover, 176 pp., 67 pictures,
$13.95, ISBN: 978-1-935902-95-9

"This fascinating book is a must-read for any Twain enthusiast"

Cornelia Dömer

MARTIN LUTHER'S TRAVEL GUIDE

500 YEARS OF THE 95 THESES. ON THE TRAIL OF THE REFORMATION IN GERMANY
ENGLISCHE AUSGABE

Softcover, 176 Seiten, 12,9 x 20,4 cm
Vollfarbe, 120 Bilder, 14 Karten
14,00 €, ISBN: 978-1-935902-44-7

Michael Brettin/Peter Kroh

BERLIN 1945

WORLD WAR II: PHOTOS OF THE AFTERMATH

From the Soviet Army Archives

Preface by Steven Kinzer

Softcover, 218 pp., 177 bw photos
$25.95, ISBN: 978-1-935902-02-7

"Even if you think you've seen it all, Berlin 1945 will surprise you"

Thomas Flemming

BERLIN IN THE COLD WAR–THE BATTLE FOR THE DIVIDED CITY

Softcover, 90 pp., $11.95
51 pictures, 3 maps
ISBN: 978-1-935902-80-5

"The story of a divided city in a nutshell, without missing a beat"

Michael Cramer

THE BERLIN WALL TODAY

REMNANTS, RUINS REMEMBRANCES

Softcover, 100 pp., $15.95
Full color, 150 pictures,
ISBN: 978-1-935902-10-2

"A well-illustrated book"